Also by Jaroslaw Jankowski

Why Are We So Different?
Your Guide to the 16 Personality Types

Why are we so very different from one another?
Why do we organise our lives in such disparate
ways? Why are our modes of assimilating
information so varied? Why are our approaches to
decision-making so diverse? Why are our forms of
relaxing and 'recharging our batteries' so dissimilar?

Your Guide to the 16 Personality Types will help you to
understand both yourselves and other people better.
It will aid you not only in avoiding any number of
traps, but also in making the most of your personal
potential, as well as in taking the right decisions
about your education and career and in building
healthy relationships with others.
The book contains the ID16™© Personality
Test, which will enable you to determine your own
personality type. It also offers a comprehensive
description of each of the sixteen types.

The Enthusiast

Your Guide
to the ENFP Personality Type

The ID16™© Personality Types series

JAROSLAW JANKOWSKI
M.Ed., EMBA

This is a book which can help you exploit your potential more fully, build healthy relationships with other people and make the right decisions about your education and career. However, it should not be considered to be a substitute for expert physiological or psychiatric consultation. Neither the author nor the publisher accept any responsibility whatsoever for any detrimental effects which may result from the inappropriate use of this book.

ID16™© is an independent typology developed by Polish educator and manager Jaroslaw Jankowski and grounded in Carl Gustav Jung's theory. It should not be confused with the personality typologies and tests proposed by other authors or offered by other institutions.

Original title: Twój typ osobowości: Entuzjasta (ENFP)
Translated from the Polish by Caryl Swift
Proof reading: Lacrosse | experts in translation
Layout editing by Zbigniew Szalbot

Published by LOGOS MEDIA

Paperback: ISBN 978-83-7981-066-6
EPUB: ISBN 978-83-7981-067-3
MOBI: ISBN 978-83-7981-068-0

Contents

Preface

The work in your hands is a compendium of knowledge on the *enthusiast*. It forms part of the *ID16™©* *Personality Types* series, which consists of sixteen books on the individual personality types and *Who Are You? The ID16™© Personality Test*, an introduction to the ID16™© independent personality typology, which is based on the theory developed by Carl Gustav Jung.

As you explore this book on the *enthusiast*, you will find the answer to a number of crucial questions:

- How do *enthusiasts* think and what do they feel? How do they make decisions? How do they solve problems? What makes them anxious? What do they fear? What irritates them?
- Which personality types are they happy to encounter on their road through life and which ones do they avoid? What kind of

friends, life partners and parents do they make? How do others perceive them?

- What are their vocational predispositions? What sort of work environment allows them to function most effectively? Which careers best suit their personality type?
- What are their strengths and what do they need to work on? How can they make the most of their potential and avoid pitfalls?
- Which famous people correspond to the *enthusiast*'s profile?

The book also contains the most essential information about the ID16™© typology.

We sincerely hope that it will help you in coming to know yourself and others better.

ID16™© and Jungian Personality Typology

ID16™© numbers among what are referred to as Jungian personality typologies, which draw on the theories developed by Carl Gustav Jung (1875-19161), a Swiss psychiatrist and psychologist and a pioneer of the 'depth psychology' approach.

On the basis of many years of research and observation, Jung came to the conclusion that the differences in people's attitudes and preferences are far from random. He developed a concept which is highly familiar to us today: the division of people into extroverts and introverts. In addition, he distinguished four personality functions, which form two opposing pairs: sensing-intuition and thinking-feeling. He also established that one function is dominant in each pair. He became convinced that each and every person's dominant functions are fixed and independent of external conditions and that, together, what they form is a personality type.

In 1938, two American psychiatrists, Horace Gray and Joseph Wheelwright, created the first personality test based on Jung's theories. It was designed to make it possible to determine the dominant functions within the three dimensions described by Jung, namely, **extraversion-introversion**, **sensing-intuition** and **thinking-feeling**. That first test became the inspiration for other researchers. In 1942, again in America, Isabel Briggs Myers and Katherine Briggs began using their own personality test, broadening Gray's and Wheelwright's classic, three-dimensional model to include a fourth: **judging-perceiving**. The majority of subsequent personality typologies and tests drawing on Jung's theories also take that fourth dimension into account. They include the American typology published by David W. Keirsey in 1978 and the personality test developed in the nineteen seventies by Aušra Augustinavičiūtė, a Lithuanian psychologist. Over the following decades, other European researchers followed in their footsteps, creating more four-dimensional personality typologies and tests for use in personal coaching and career counselling.

ID16TM© figures among that group. An independent typology developed by Polish educator and manager Jaroslaw Jankowski, it was published in the first decade of the twenty-first century. ID16TM© is based on Carl Jung's classic theory and, like other contemporary Jungian typologies, it follows a four-dimensional path, terming those dimensions the **four natural inclinations**. These inclinations are dichotomous in nature and the picture they provide gives us information regarding a person's personality type. Analysis of the first inclination is intended to determine the dominant **source of life energy**, this being either the exterior or the interior world. Analysis of the second inclination defines the dominant **mode of assimilating information**, which occurs via the senses or via intuition. Analysis of the third inclination supplies a description of the **decision-making mode**, where either mind or heart is dominant, while analysis of the fourth inclination produces a definition of the dominant **lifestyle** as either organised or spontaneous. The combination of all these natural inclinations results in **sixteen possible personality types**.

One remarkable feature of the ID16™© typology is its practical dimension. It describes the individual personality types in action – at work, in daily life and in interpersonal relations. It neither concentrates on the internal dynamics of personality nor does it undertake any theoretical attempts at explaining or commenting on invisible, interior processes. The focus is turned more toward the ways in which a given personality type manifests itself externally and how it affects the surrounding world. This emphasis on the social aspect of personality places ID16™© somewhat closer to the previously mentioned typology developed by Aušra Augustinavičiūtė.

Each of the ID16™© personality types is the result of a given person's natural inclinations. There is nothing evaluative or judgemental about ascribing a person to a given type, though. No particular personality type is 'better' or 'worse' than any other. Each type is quite simply different and each has its own potential strengths and weaknesses. ID16™© makes it possible to identify and describe those differences. It helps us to understand ourselves and discover our place in the world.

Familiarity with our personality profile enables us to make full use of our potential and work on the areas which might cause us trouble. It is an invaluable aid in everyday life, in solving problems, in building healthy relationships with other people and in making decisions relating to our education and careers.

Determining personality is a process which is neither arbitrary nor mechanical in nature. As the 'owner and user' of our personality, each and every one of us is fully capable of defining which type we belong to. The individual's role is thus pivotal. This self-identification can be achieved either by analysing the descriptions of the ID16™© personality types and steadily narrowing down the fields of choice or by taking the short cut provided by the ID16™© Personality Test.[1] The role played by each 'personality user' is equally crucial when it comes to the test, given that the outcome depends entirely on the answers they provide.

Identifying personality types helps us to know both ourselves and others. Nonetheless, it should not be treated as some kind of future-determining oracle. No personality type can ever justify our weaknesses or poor interpersonal relationships. It might, however, help us to understand their causes!

ID16™© treats personality type not as a static, genetic, pre-determined condition, but as a product

---

[1] The test can be found in *Why Are We So Different? Your Guide to the 16 Personality Types* by Jaroslaw Jankowski.

of innate and acquired characteristics. As such, it is a concept which neither diminishes free will nor engages in pigeonholing people. What it does is open up new perspectives for us, encouraging us to work on ourselves and indicating the areas where that work is most needed.

The Enthusiast (ENFP)

THE ID16™© PERSONALITY TYPOLOGY

The Personality in a Nutshell

Life motto: We'll manage!

In brief, *enthusiasts* …

are energetic, enthusiastic and optimistic. Capable of enjoying life and looking ahead to the future, they are dynamic, quick-witted and creative. They have a liking for people in general, value honest and genuine relationships and are warm, sincere and emotional. Criticism is something they handle badly. With their gift for empathy and ability to perceive people's needs, feelings and motives, they both inspire others and infect them with their own enthusiasm.

They love to be at the centre of events and are flexible and capable of improvising. Their inclination leads towards idealistic notions. Being easily distracted, they have problems with seeing things through to the end.

The *enthusiast's* four natural inclinations:

- source of life energy: the exterior world
- mode of assimilating information: intuition
- decision-making mode: the heart
- lifestyle: spontaneous

Similar personality types:

- the Counsellor
- the Idealist
- the Mentor

Statistical data:

- *enthusiasts* constitute between five and eight per cent of the global community
- women predominate among *enthusiasts* (60 per cent)
- Italy is an example of a nation corresponding to the *enthusiast's* profile[2]

The Four-Letter Code

In terms of Jungian personality typology, the universal four-letter code for the *enthusiast* is ENFP.

---

[2] What this means is not that all the residents of Italy fall within this personality type, but that Italian society as a whole possesses a great many of the character traits typical of the *enthusiast*.

General character traits

Enthusiasts love life and have the ability to enjoy every moment. Wherever the action is, that is where *enthusiasts* like to be. Optimists by nature, they view the future with hope and have faith in people. They like change and fresh experiences and constantly hunger to explore new concepts, discover new places and meet new people.

Enthusiasts will always make an effort to be at the centre of things and they need contact with other people. When they are condemned to being alone and cut off from the world, they descend into a state of apathy. They value good relationships with other people and the liking of those around them matters a great deal to them. Nonetheless, it is not something they will pursue at any price, such as behaving in a way which flies in the face of their convictions. They dislike being subjected to pressure, controlled, checked on and pigeonholed and, by the same token, they themselves respect the freedom and independence of others.

Perception and thinking

Enthusiasts are curious about the world, constantly seek fresh sources of inspiration and are usually interested in new concepts and stimulating ideas. They have no difficulty in assimilating complex notions and abstract theories. Their approach to problems and tasks is creative and often innovative. Once they have identified the connections between disparate facts and occurrences, they are quicker than most to reach a solution. They will sometimes discern hidden meanings and signs in the events and situations around them. As a rule, they are original, inventive and orientated towards the future and are also characterised by incredible optimism and enthusiasm ... hence the name for this personality type.

Their attitude inspires others and gives them faith that they will succeed, while they themselves are usually firmly convinced that any venture they undertake will prosper. Obstacles and setbacks thus have no power to perturb or discourage them. When they are aware that an opportunity has appeared, they are ready to take a risk and launch themselves into uncharted waters, just as long as there is a chance of making the most of it. Indeed, they find the very thought of unexploited chances difficult to bear.

Attitude to others

Enthusiasts have an ability to influence other people's behaviour and even to manipulate them. They usually put this skill to positive use in encouraging others to discover their talents, for instance, or motivating them to act or building up their faith in themselves.

When they tackle problems, they are capable of getting to the crux of the matter without being deceived by outward appearances or illusions. They are characterised by their remarkable empathy, which enables them to read other people's feelings, emotions and even their hidden motives, to say nothing of the fact that they are often capable of describing someone else's situation, feelings and needs better than that person can themselves. On occasion, they may well take on the role of 'spokesperson' for others. As many people see it, their extraordinary interpersonal skills, such as their ability to fathom out someone else's secrets, seem to verge on the magical. There is nothing supernatural involved, though: *enthusiasts'* intuition is, quite simply, highly developed and they are masterly observers, paying attention not only to words, but also to non-verbal signals.

Helping others is a source of enormous joy to them and they are genuinely delighted when, thanks to their assistance, people begin to make the most of their potential and gain faith in their own powers. On the other hand, when their efforts fail to produce results or when people are either unwilling or unable to avail themselves of their own possibilities, they will be thoroughly downcast.

They are not reclusive by nature; other people are a part of their lives and thus occupy a great deal of their thoughts. As a rule, they excel at reading people's emotions and feelings – even from afar! When they read a letter or e-mail from someone they know, they are able to put themselves in their shoes, imagining what they are going through and how they are feeling. They will frequently put other people's needs before their own.

As others see them

Enthusiasts' sincerity, warmth and genuine interest acts on others like a magnet, although some people are irritated by their talkativeness and their extreme optimism, which is sometimes taken for naïvety, as well as by their unpunctuality and unreliability.

While it is, indeed, true that, on occasion, they may fail to keep their word, this is neither a conscious action nor is it the deliberate disrespect which some people consider it to be. *Enthusiasts* never make a promise while actually having every intention of breaking it. However, what does happen is that they become so excited by fresh challenges that they are quite capable of completely forgetting their previous undertakings and giving themselves over entirely to new ones, until the next fresh stimulus comes along. At times, this attitude can mean that they are labelled as unreliable, chaotic and lacking in substance.

Enthusiasts themselves are irritated by unnatural behaviour and find it difficult to understand the reasons for which some people try to pretend to be someone other than they are. Passiveness, scepticism and chronic pessimism also set their teeth on edge and they simply cannot comprehend those who are always moaning and complaining about everything, and who invariably take a critical stance towards new ideas and concepts.

Decisions

When *enthusiasts* are faced with making decisions, they will happily turn to others for their opinion, listen to their advice and avail themselves of their experience. In general, they rely on the views of experts and widely acknowledged authorities. They operate on the basis of both their usually unerring intuition and their remarkable 'feel' for a situation. The way in which a given decision or action will be received by those around them is something they never fail to bear in mind, as is its impact on other people. Indeed, not only are they incapable of proceeding without giving due consideration to the human factor, but they also mistrust those who claim to rely solely on hard data and facts.

Organisational modes

In *enthusiasts*, the force driving them to act is, of course, their enthusiasm! They frequently view the world through rose-tinted glasses and fail to discern potential dangers. As a result, they are liable to involve themselves in hazardous ventures and undertake risky activities. Being highly spontaneous and flexible, it is unusual for them to devote overmuch time to deliberation and preparation; once an idea strikes them, they are far more likely to launch into action as soon as they can. On the whole, they cope better with a number of smaller undertakings than with one substantial task demanding months of systematic work and, in general, they have no liking for routine and repetitive activities such as paperwork, cleaning and shopping, perceiving them as restricting, burdensome and a waste of time which would be better spent doing more exciting and creative things.

Enthusiasts are not the best of organisers and planners and their actions tend to be more impulse-led. They often have difficulties in making the best use of their time, as well as in managing money, and their financial situation can often be unstable. It might happen that they will spend large sums on luxury items, only to find themselves needing to borrow money to buy the staples. They are also readier than many to reach for their credit cards.

Communication

Enthusiasts are excellent oral communicators and will readily join in conversations and discussions when they are with a group of people. Speaking in public presents them with no major problems and they are capable of expressing challenging issues clearly and comprehensibly, often bringing interesting stories and colourful examples into play when they do. They also have the gift of persuasion and are capable of convincing others that they are right.

Amongst their friends and acquaintances, they take a delight in telling jokes and amusing stories about their own lives, often with added embellishments! What they have to say brims with emotion and enthusiasm, leading many of their listeners to envy them their adventures and vibrantly fascinating lives. On the other hand, they are frequently wholly unaware of the fact that they might well be dominating a discussion or even, quite simply, taking it over entirely and not letting anyone else get a word in edgeways. On the contrary: even when they are delivering what is, in fact, a monologue, they can be under the impression that they are having an amazing conversation. Their loquaciousness can be another problem, since they are capable of talking for hours on end, holding forth in a veritable river of words, which is something that other people can find fairly unbearable.

In the face of stress

Situations of conflict are often a source of stress to *enthusiasts*, as are displays of indifference or criticism from others. During prolonged periods of tension, they can sometimes become stubborn or start suspecting other people of wishing them ill. Fortunately, though, they are also capable of relaxing 'to the max' and completely wiping their problems, responsibilities and obligations from their minds when they go into 'time-out mode'.

In general, they prefer active leisure pursuits and also greatly enjoy family and social get-togethers, to say nothing of happily organising them themselves.

At times, they will try and unload their stress by turning to substances or thrill-seeking.

Socially

Enthusiasts are quick to strike up new acquaintanceships and are extremely outgoing and approachable. As a result, other people will often feel as if they have known them for ages when, in fact, they have really only just met. Highly flexible in their contact with others, they do all they can to respond to their needs, sometimes neglecting their own in the process. All of these characteristics mean that other people feel good in their company.

Enthusiasts themselves love being in the midst of people and the acknowledgement, acceptance and interest of others matters a great deal to them. They approach their interpersonal relationships with extraordinary enthusiasm and have the ability to amuse people and shower them with praise, to say nothing of adding a *soupçon* of coquetry to their dealings with others. However, they also display uncanny intuition, tact and empathy, knowing exactly how to behave in a given situation and possessing the ability to adapt to the circumstances and emotional state of others.

They are eager to meet new people and, with their thirst for bonds which are both genuine and absolute, they have a tendency to seek ideals in terms of the 'perfect friend', or the 'perfect partner for life'. Good relations with others are highly important to them and they will do everything in their power to prevent conflict from raising its head. In general, they are incapable of consciously criticising other people; indeed, they will even struggle when it comes to voicing a critical opinion about someone else's views or calling attention to their inappropriate behaviour, preferring in general to remain silent about the problem and stifle their own negative emotions.

Enthusiasts find indifference and silence on the part of others very hard to bear. They are incapable both of understanding behaviour of that kind and of coping with it. As a rule, they assume, entirely wrongly, that a lack of reaction signifies hostility.

Amongst friends

Enthusiasts prize honest and genuine relationships. Meeting new people, talking to friends and acquaintances and spending time with them make up the essence of their lives, which lose all colour and savour when they are cut off from others.

They are very quick to read other people and, after no more than a few minutes of conversation with someone, will often know that they are simply not on the same wavelength and that a mutual understanding is never really going to happen. Their relationships with others are of the highest importance to them. They usually have a host of friends and acquaintances and are the life and soul of any gathering. People are eager to spend time with them, since *enthusiasts* brim with positive energy and humour, as well as being deeply sincere, showing warmth towards others, respecting their individualism and setting store by their needs. Their acquaintanceships are highly intense, but tend to be short-lived; when they meet new people, they turn the full beam of their attention and energy onto them and will sometimes forget those who came before.

With their outgoing nature, they usually express their emotions openly and are unstinting in their praise of others. They have difficulty in striking up a friendship with people who are disinclined to externalise their feelings or to say what they think and often take that kind of behaviour as a sign of dislike. A cold, unfriendly and inescapable environment, such as a workplace, will cause them enormous discomfort and strain. They find spending time with acquaintances, friends and family the best way to relieve stress.

Enthusiasts are almost always surrounded by people and have a host of friends and acquaintances, although the majority of these relationships are superficial in nature. So many things attract their attention and they are so easily distracted that even their closest acquaintances often feel as if they will never have them entirely to themselves. As a rule, *enthusiasts* have only a few really close friends. They most frequently tend to be *counsellors*, *idealists*, *presenters* or other *enthusiasts* and, most rarely, *inspectors*, *administrators* and *practitioners*.

As life partners

Enthusiasts make highly devoted and caring partners, bringing warmth, enthusiasm, creativity and a sense of humour to their relationships. Their partner's happiness and well-being matter greatly to them and they do all they can to meet their needs, showing them enormous warmth and unstintingly offering them tender words and affectionate gestures.

They, too, need warmth, closeness and acceptance and, given that they are profoundly affected by any kind of cutting remark, unflattering comment or even indifference on the part of their nearest and dearest, they are easily hurt. However, since discussing tough and unpleasant issues is anathema to them, they will try to avoid conflicts and arguments at any price, much preferring to suffer rather than tell their partner that something has upset or distressed them. They will thus often be incapable of withdrawing from bad or destructive relationships.

Enthusiasts keep a constant eye on the state of their relationships and are quick to sense problems. When they do crop up, the *enthusiast* partner will be deeply affected by them and will also feel responsible for them. By the same token, if the relationship ends, they will often reproach themselves for not having done everything within their power to save it. As a rule, they take their responsibilities very seriously, although it can happen that they themselves are the cause of their relationship troubles, since their love of change and experimenting, their dreams of 'perfect love' and their aversion to routine might lead them to seek experiences outside their partnership, this being a particular danger when their 'other half' does not share their fascinations, enthusiasm and curiosity about the world. On the other hand, their care for those they love and their deeply rooted values have an enormous bearing on the permanence of their relationships.

The natural candidates for an *enthusiast's* life partner are people of a personality type akin to their own; *counsellors, idealists* or *mentors*. Building mutual understanding and harmonious relations will be easier in a union of that kind. Nonetheless, experience has taught us that people are also capable of creating happy and successful relationships despite what would seem to be an evident typological incompatibility. Moreover, the differences between two partners can lend added dynamics to a relationship and engender personal development. Indeed, for many people, this is a prospect that appears more attractive than the vision of a harmonious relationship in which concord and full, mutual understanding hold sway.

As parents

Enthusiasts take their parental responsibilities extremely seriously. They nurture their offspring's development and pass on the values which they themselves believe in, surround them with warmth, give them faith in their own powers and are unstinting in their affection and praise. At times, their older children, in particular, might well quite simply feel embarrassed by the love and tenderness their *enthusiast* parent lavishes on them, especially in front of their peers. Nonetheless, they appreciate the fact that they can always count on their spiritual and emotional support in difficult moments.

Enthusiasts' inborn aversion to repetitive and routine activities means that helping their children with everyday tasks of a practical nature, such as their homework, presents them with a considerable challenge. Nonetheless, in the majority of cases, their concern for their offspring's well-being wins through and they are able to force themselves to do the kind of tasks they have little liking for.

Their nature usually has something of the child about it and they are great partners-in-fun to their children. They love games, adventures and all kinds of experiments, so 'fun time' spent together is an attraction not only for their offspring, but for the *enthusiast* parents themselves. In turn, their inconsistency and changeability are a source of problems, as they switch from being extremely easy-going and understanding one day to stern and impatient the next, an approach which sometimes means that their children are unable to grasp the behavioural model their parent is following and lose their sense of stability and security. *Enthusiasts* also frequently have problems with disciplining their offspring and ensuring that they do what they are supposed to. However, things are radically different if their children's behaviour violates the principles they themselves profess. When that happens, their reaction will be swift, for *enthusiasts* firmly believe that there are boundaries which should never be crossed.

Once adults, their children have fond memories of the carefree fun they had with their *enthusiast* parent and of the warm and loving atmosphere of their childhood home. They also appreciate the way they respected their choices, demonstrated their support and taught them to care about other people.

Work and career paths

Enthusiasts succeed in all sorts of professions which are as different as chalk and cheese. They usually have a wealth of professional experience, since many of them change jobs relatively frequently and may well switch sectors several times over the course of their working lives. They are most attracted to work which offers possibilities for creativity, experimenting and solving problems. On the other hand, they cannot bear bureaucracy, hierarchies, routine, repetitive tasks and rigid procedures and find cold, hierarchical and formalised corporate environments very hard to handle.

Tasks

Enthusiasts will throw themselves into tasks which provide practical opportunities to give voice to their convictions and put the values they hold dear into effect. They fit in well in institutions geared towards the good of society and bringing about tangible and positive changes in the life of the local community or the country or on a global scale, since they like knowing that their activities have a positive impact on other people's lives and help them to solve their problems. When they are working on a task in which they believe, they will invest all their energy in it, so there will be no need to supervise or motivate them. However, kick-starting them into action on jobs they find tedious or which are inconsistent with their system of values will prove rather a challenge. They also have no liking for working individually and, in professional terms, their worst-case scenario would be a 'static' job, performed alone and demanding long-term focus on a single task. What they enjoy is team work providing movement, variety and frequent change.

Skills and stumbling blocks

Enthusiasts cope excellently with tasks demanding interpersonal skills, inventiveness, flexibility and the ability to improvise. They gravitate towards the action, wherever it might be. In general, they are a pillar of support to their colleagues, readily doing all they can to meet their needs and successfully building compromises. On the one hand, they are highly inventive and creative; on the other, they are quick to become bored and have difficulty in continuing with a task they have already begun once a new and more interesting project appears on the horizon. They often have trouble organising their time, determining their priorities and focusing on what they should be doing. Their propensity is to be easily distracted and, in the battle for their attention, it is usually the newest and most powerful stimulus that will emerge victorious. Uniformity and bureaucracy irritate them immensely and they will sometimes rebel openly against burdensome procedures and regulations which they consider to be unrealistic or impractical. They also find apathy, lethargy, stagnation and passiveness hard to handle.

When working as part of a team, *enthusiasts* value a healthy and friendly atmosphere, feeling themselves to be on very uncertain ground indeed in situations of conflict and struggles for power or authority. They cannot comprehend people who are capable of harming others in their fight for their own interests and find the motives for acting in that manner inconceivable – it is simply not their world.

Views on workplace hierarchy

Enthusiasts appreciate superiors who are flexible and open to innovative solutions and who point their subordinates in the general direction they should take, but afford them freedom in accomplishing their tasks and respect their individual style of working. They favour democratic management principles and give their esteem to bosses who take the employees' opinions into account and give them the opportunity to take part in making decisions which are crucial to the organisation.

Enthusiasts also have natural leadership skills. Where they go, others will follow, inspired and motivated by them. Their enthusiasm and faith in the success of shared undertakings is infectious and they help others to look at problems from a wider perspective and identify future opportunities. Their leadership is grounded in their ability both to identify people's predispositions correctly and to trust them; keeping an iron hand on the reins is not a style they favour. With their knowledge of who will cope best with a given job, they are able to allocate the right tasks to the right person.

In positions at the top of the tree, their management methods involve assistance from other people. At the same time, they avoid unnecessary bureaucracy, prefer a natural, informal approach and will often consult their subordinates about critical decisions. However, they run into problems when it comes to disciplining poor employees, as well as frequently failing to keep their word, which arouses their subordinates' frustration. *Enthusiast* bosses are at their most effective when they can avail themselves of help from assistants who will take on their administrative burden, keep a firm eye on their deadlines and provide them with the support they need in managing their time.

Professions

Knowledge of our own personality profile and natural preferences provides us with invaluable help in choosing the optimal path in our professional careers. Experience has shown that, while *enthusiasts* are perfectly able to work and find fulfilment in a range of fields, their personality type naturally predisposes them to the following fields and professions:

- acting
- advisor
- artistic director
- clergy
- consultant
- diplomat
- editor
- entrepreneur
- events organiser
- insurance agent
- interior designer
- journalist
- manager
- mediator
- musician
- painter
- paramedic
- politician
- psychiatrist
- psychologist
- public relations
- reporter
- sales assistant
- sales representative
- scientist
- speech therapist
- social welfare
- teacher
- therapist
- writer

Potential strengths and weaknesses

Like any other personality type, *enthusiasts* have their potential strengths and weaknesses and this potential can be cultivated in a variety of ways. *Enthusiasts'* personal happiness and professional fulfilment depend on whether they make the most of the 'pluses' offered by their personality type and face up to its inherent dangers. Here, then, is a SUMMARY of those 'pluses' and dangers:

Potential strengths

Enthusiasts are energetic and optimistic. With their positive attitude to other people and sensitivity to their needs, they emanate warmth and sincerity. As a result, they draw others to themselves naturally and people feel good in their company. They have the ability to read human emotions, feelings and motives, obvious and hidden alike, and are quick to discern who they are dealing with. Their intuition is superb and they display an uncanny tact and 'feel' for others in their interpersonal relationships, knowing exactly how to behave in a given situation and having the ability to build compromises. They are tolerant and accept others, respecting their freedom and independence.

Being flexible and possessing the ability to improvise, they cope extremely well with change and respond rapidly to new circumstances. Versatile, nimble-witted and creative, they are quick to assimilate complex concepts and abstract theories. Their oral communication skills are excellent and they are able to express their own thoughts clearly, as well as having impressive powers of persuasion. They are unperturbed by obstacles and setbacks and have no fear of experiments or innovative methods for solving problems. Their thinking is global; they are able to identify the connections between disparate phenomena and look at the bigger picture when considering problems. They have natural leadership skills and are capable of motivating and inspiring people, as well as infecting them with their optimism and faith in their success, drawing out the best in them and helping them to make the most of their potential. Accepting help from others and availing themselves of their experience also present them with no problems.

Potential weaknesses

Enthusiasts often have trouble with determining their priorities and focusing on carrying out their tasks. As a rule, they launch into a job enthusiastically, but are easily distracted and seeing it through to the end is something of a challenge to them. They may well fail to keep their word or meet deadlines and have a tendency to put off doing what has to be done. Managing their time is another problem area for them, as is planning, and they also struggle mightily with repetitive, everyday activities and routine duties in both their private and their working lives. Be it cleaning and shopping or be it compiling reports and accounts, their efforts, such as they are, will probably be dismal.

They are unable to appreciate constructive criticism or benefit from it and will normally perceive it as an attack on themselves personally or an attempt to discredit their values. Being highly dependent on the opinions of others, they cope very badly with unflattering comments and cutting remarks and will also go to any lengths to avoid conflicts and disagreeable conversations, preferring, on the whole, to keep quiet about a problem rather than confront it.

Voicing critical opinions and calling other people's attention to shortcomings or inappropriate behaviour is difficult for them and they tend to clamp the lid down on their negative emotions. In focusing on other people's needs, they often forget about their own, and since they incline towards being over-trusting they will sometimes be used by others. With their enthusiasm and propensity for viewing the world through rose-tinted glasses, they can lose touch with reality on occasion, fail to view potential threats seriously enough and display a tendency to take excessive risks.

Personal development

Enthusiasts' personal development depends on the extent to which they make use of their natural potential and surmount the dangers inherent in their personality type. What follows are some practical indicators which, together, form a specific guide that we might call *The Enthusiast's Ten Commandments.*

Keep your focus fixed

Determine your priorities and make a serious effort to finish what you undertake. Keep your eyes firmly fixed on the most crucial tasks and stop letting yourself be distracted by less important matters. Do that and you will find yourself avoiding frustration and achieving more.

Be more practical

You have a natural inclination to come up with idealistic notions which sometimes have little in common with real life. Give some thought to the practical aspects and to how they can actually be accomplished in this imperfect world we live in.

Stop fearing criticism

Quell your fear of expressing your own critical opinions and of accepting criticism from others. Criticism can be constructive. There is no law which says that it has to mean attacking people or undermining their worth.

Stop blaming others for your problems

Who has the greatest influence over your life? Who is the person most competent to solve your problems? You, of course! Shift your focus away from external obstacles, setbacks and adversities and concentrate on your strengths and making the most of your potential instead.

Stop agonising over the plan and get going on the action

Instead of nit-picking over how you can improve on what you intend to do, simply get going and do it. Otherwise the day will come when you realise that you have spent your entire life perfecting your plans. Surely setting out to accomplish them and doing things well, but not necessarily to the point of sheer perfection, would be better than never doing anything at all?

Give some thought to yourself

Give some consideration to your own needs and find the time to reflect on your own life. Stop letting yourself be used and start learning to say 'no'. If you really want to help other people effectively, you also have to look after yourself.

Stop being afraid of conflict

Conflicts do arise sometimes, even in our closest circles. They need not necessarily be destructive, though. In fact, they very often help us to identify problems and solve them! So, when conflicts emerge, stop hiding your head in the sand and, instead, express your point of view and feelings about the situation openly.

Ask

Stop assuming that, if other people are silent, it means that they are indifferent or hostile. If you really want to know what they think, ask them.

Stop fearing ideas and opinions which are different from yours

Before you reject them, give them some consideration and try to understand them. Being open to the viewpoints of others is not synonymous with discarding your own.

Give voice to your negative emotions

Stop suppressing your irritation, vexation and anger. If a situation or other people's behaviour exasperates you, then say so. The benefits will be twofold. Not only will you help them to understand what upsets you, but you will also help yourself to avoid self-destruction and vehement, uncontrolled reactions.

Well-known figures

Below is a list of some well-known people who match the *enthusiast's* profile:

- **Joseph Haydn** (1732-1809); an Austrian composer of the Classical period and the first of the three who are often referred to jointly as the First Viennese School.
- **Mark Twain**, (Samuel Langhorne Clemens; 1835-1910); an American writer of Scottish origins whose works include *The Adventures of Tom Sawyer* and its sequel, *The Adventures of Huckleberry Finn.*
- **Edith Wharton** (1862-1937); an American writer whose works include *The Age of Innocence.*
- **James Dobson** (born in 1936); an American Christian psychologist and the author of numerous books, including *What Wives Wish Their Husbands Knew About Women.*
- **Cher** (Cherilyn Sarkisian LaPierre; born in 1946); an American singer of Armenian-Cherokee ancestry, she also operates in many other capacities in the entertainment industry.
- **Jonathan Pryce** (Jonathan Price; born in 1947); a Welsh stage and screen actor whose movies include *Pirates of the Caribbean.*
- **James Woods** (born in 1947); an American screen actor whose movies include *Salvador,* he is also a screenwriter and director.

- **Gregg Henry** (born in 1952); an American stage and screen actor whose films include *Body Double*, he is also a musician and singer.
- **Carrie Fisher** (1956-2016); an American screen actress whose filmography includes *Star Wars*.
- **Damon Hill** (born in 1960); a retired British racing driver and former Formula 1 world champion.
- **Heather Locklear** (born in 1961); an American screen actress whose filmography includes the TV series *Dynasty*.
- **Sandra Bullock** (born in 1964); an American screen actress whose filmography includes *While You Were Sleeping*, she is also a producer.
- **Keanu Reeves** (born in 1964); a Canadian film actor whose filmography includes *Matrix*, he is also a director, producer, musician and author.
- **Jason Statham** (born in 1972); an English film actor whose filmography includes *The Transporter*, he is also a producer, martial artist and former competition diver.

The ID16™© Personality Types in a Nutshell

The Administrator (ESTJ)

Life motto: We'll get the job done!

Administrators are hard-working, responsible and extremely loyal. Energetic and decisive, they value order, stability, security and clear rules. They are matter-of-fact and businesslike, logical, rational and practical and possess the capability to assimilate large amounts of detailed information.

Superb organisers, they are intolerant of ineffectuality, wastefulness and slothfulness. True to their convictions and direct in their contact with others, they present their point of view decisively and openly express critical opinions, sometimes hurting other people as a result.

The *administrator*'s four natural inclinations:

- source of life energy: the exterior world
- mode of assimilating information: via the senses
- decision-making mode: the mind
- lifestyle: organised

Similar personality types:

- the Animator
- the Inspector
- the Practitioner

Statistical data:

- *administrators* constitute between ten and thirteen per cent of the global community
- men predominate among *administrators* (60 per cent)
- the United States is an example of a nation corresponding to the *administrator's* profile[3]

Find out more!

The Administrator. Your Guide to the ESTJ Personality Type by Jaroslaw Jankowski

---

[3] What this means is not that all the residents of the USA fall within this personality type, but that American society as a whole possesses a great many of the character traits typical of the *administrator.*

The Advocate (ESFJ)

Life motto: How can I help you?

Advocates are well-organised, energetic and enthusiastic. Practical, responsible and conscientious, they are sincere and exceptionally gregarious.

Advocates are perceptive of human feelings, emotions and needs. They value harmony and find criticism and conflict difficult to bear. With their sensitivity to any and every manifestation of injustice, prejudice or detriment to another, they are genuinely interested in other people's problems and take real delight in helping them and tending to their needs, while often neglecting their own. They have a tendency to do everything for others and can be vulnerable to manipulation.

The *advocate*'s four natural inclinations:

- source of life energy: the exterior world
- mode of assimilating information: via the senses
- decision-making mode: the heart
- lifestyle: organised

Similar personality types:

- the Presenter
- the Protector
- the Artist

Statistical data:

- *advocates* constitute between ten and thirteen per cent of the global community

- women predominate among *advocates* (70 per cent)
- Canada is an example of a nation corresponding to the *advocate's* profile

Find out more!

The Advocate. Your Guide to the ESFJ Personality Type by Jaroslaw Jankowski

The Animator (ESTP)

Life motto: Let's DO something!

Animators are energetic, active and enterprising. Fond of the company of others, they have the ability to enjoy the moment and are spontaneous, flexible and open to change.

Animators are inspirers and instigators, spurring others to act. Being logical, rational and pragmatic realists, they are wearied by abstract concepts and solutions for the future. Their focus is on solving concrete problems in the here and now. They have difficulties with organising and planning and can be impulsive, acting first and thinking later.

The *animator's* four natural inclinations:

- source of life energy: the exterior world
- mode of assimilating information: via the senses
- decision-making mode: the mind
- lifestyle: spontaneous

Similar personality types:

- the Administrator
- the Practitioner
- the Inspector

Statistical data:

- *animators* constitute between six and ten per cent of the global community
- men predominate among *animators* (60 per cent)
- Australia is an example of a nation corresponding to the *animator's* profile

Find out more!

The Animator. Your Guide to the ESTP Personality Type by Jaroslaw Jankowski

The Artist (ISFP)

Life motto: Let's create something!

Artists are sensitive, creative and original, with a sense of the aesthetic and natural artistic talents. Independent in character, they follow their own system of values and are optimistic in outlook, with a positive approach to life and an ability to enjoy the moment.

Helping others is a source of joy to them. They find abstract theories tedious and would rather create reality than talk about it, although starting on something new comes more easily to them than finishing what they have already started. They have difficulty in voicing their own desires and needs.

The *artist's* four natural inclinations:

- source of life energy: the interior world
- mode of assimilating information: via the senses
- decision-making mode: the heart
- lifestyle: spontaneous

Similar personality types:

- the Protector
- the Presenter
- the Advocate

Statistical data:

- *artists* constitute between six and nine per cent of the global community
- women predominate among *artists* (60 per cent)
- China is an example of a nation corresponding to the *artist's* profile

Find out more!

The Artist. Your Guide to the ISFP Personality Type by Jaroslaw Jankowski

The Counsellor (ENFJ)

Life motto: My friends are my world

Counsellors are optimistic, enthusiastic and quick-witted. Courteous and tactful, they have an extraordinary gift for empathy and find joy in acting for the good of others, with no thought of themselves. They have the ability to influence other people, inspiring them, eliciting their hidden potential and giving them faith in their own powers. Radiating warmth, they draw others to them and often help them in solving their personal problems.

Counsellors can be over-trusting and have a tendency to view the world through rose-tinted glasses. With their focus on other people, they often forget about their own needs.

The *counsellor's* four natural inclinations:

- source of life energy: the exterior world
- mode of assimilating information: intuition
- decision-making mode: the heart
- lifestyle: organised

Similar personality types:

- the Enthusiast
- the Mentor
- the Idealist

Statistical data:

- *counsellors* constitute between three and five per cent of the global community
- women predominate among *counsellors* (80 per cent)
- France is an example of a nation corresponding to the *counsellor's* profile

Find out more!

The Counsellor. Your Guide to the ENFJ Personality Type by Jaroslaw Jankowski

The Director (ENTJ)

Life motto: I'll tell you what you need to do.

Directors are independent, active and decisive. Rational, logical and creative, when they analyse problems they look at the wider picture and are able to foresee the future consequences of human activities. They are characterised by optimism and a healthy sense of their own worth and are capable of transforming theoretical concepts into concrete, practical plans of action.

Visionaries, mentors and organisers, *directors* possess natural leadership skills. Their powerful personalities and direct and critical style can often have an intimidating effect, causing them problems in their interpersonal relationships.

The *director's* four natural inclinations:

- source of life energy: the exterior world
- mode of assimilating information: intuition
- decision-making mode: the mind
- lifestyle: organised

Similar personality types:

- the Innovator
- the Strategist
- the Logician

Statistical data:

- *directors* constitute between two and five per cent of the global community
- men predominate among *directors* (70 per cent)

- Holland is an example of a nation corresponding to the *director's* profile

Find out more!

The Director. Your Guide to the ENTJ Personality Type by Jaroslaw Jankowski

The Enthusiast (ENFP)

Life motto: We'll manage!

Enthusiasts are energetic, enthusiastic and optimistic. Capable of enjoying life and looking ahead to the future, they are dynamic, quick-witted and creative. They have a liking for people in general, value honest and genuine relationships and are warm, sincere and emotional. Criticism is something they handle badly. With their gift for empathy and ability to perceive people's needs, feelings and motives, they both inspire others and infect them with their own enthusiasm.

They love to be at the centre of events and are flexible and capable of improvising. Their inclination leads towards idealistic notions. Being easily distracted, they have problems with seeing things through to the end.

The *enthusiast's* four natural inclinations:

- source of life energy: the exterior world
- mode of assimilating information: intuition
- decision-making mode: the heart
- lifestyle: spontaneous

Similar personality types:

- the Counsellor
- the Idealist
- the Mentor

Statistical data:

- *enthusiasts* constitute between five and eight per cent of the global community
- women predominate among *enthusiasts* (60 per cent)
- Italy is an example of a nation corresponding to the *enthusiast's* profile

Find out more!

The Enthusiast. Your Guide to the ENFP Personality Type by Jaroslaw Jankowski

The Idealist (INFP)

Life motto: We CAN live differently.

Idealists are sensitive, loyal, and creative. Living in accordance with the values they hold is of immense importance to them and they both manifest an interest in the reality of the spirit and delve deeply into the mysteries of life. Wrapped up in the world's problems and open to the needs of other people, they prize harmony and balance.

Idealists are romantic; not only are they able to show love, but they also need warmth and affection themselves. With their outstanding ability to read other people's feelings and emotions, they build healthy, profound and enduring relationships. They feel that they are on very shaky ground in situations of conflict and have no real resistance to stress and criticism.

The *idealist's* four natural inclinations:

- source of life energy: the interior world
- mode of assimilating information: intuition
- decision-making mode: the heart
- lifestyle: spontaneous

Similar personality types:

- the Mentor
- the Enthusiast
- the Counsellor

Statistical data:

- *idealists* constitute between one and four per cent of the global community
- women predominate among *idealists* (60 per cent)
- Thailand is an example of a nation corresponding to the *idealist's* profile

Find out more!

The Idealist. Your Guide to the INFP Personality Type by Jaroslaw Jankowski

The Innovator (ENTP)

Life motto: How about trying a different approach…?

Innovators are inventive, original and independent. Optimistic, energetic and enterprising, they are people of action who love being at the centre of events and solving 'insoluble' problems. Their thoughts are turned to the future and they are curious about the world and visionary by nature. Open to new concepts and ideas, they enjoy new experiences and experiments and have the ability to identify the connections between separate events.

Innovators are spontaneous, communicative and self-assured. However, they tend to overestimate their own possibilities and have problems with seeing things through to the end. They are also inclined to be impatient and to take risks.

The *innovator's* four natural inclinations:

- source of life energy: the exterior world
- mode of assimilating information: intuition
- decision-making mode: the mind
- lifestyle: spontaneous

Similar personality types:

- the Director
- the Logician
- the Strategist

Statistical data:

- *innovators* constitute between three and five per cent of the global community

- men predominate among *innovators* (70 per cent)
- Israel is an example of a nation corresponding to the *innovator's* profile

Find out more!

The Innovator. Your Guide to the ENTP Personality Type by Jaroslaw Jankowski

The Inspector (ISTJ)

Life motto: *Duty first.*

Inspectors are people who can always be counted on. Well-mannered, punctual, reliable, conscientious and responsible, when they give their word, they keep it. Being analytical, methodical, systematic and logical by nature, they tend be seen as serious, cold and reserved. They prize calm, stability and order, have no fondness for change and like clear principles and concrete rules.

Inspectors are hard-working, persevering and capable of seeing things through to the end. As perfectionists, they try to exercise control over everything within their sphere and are sparing in their praise. They also underrate the importance of other people's feelings and emotions.

The *inspector's* four natural inclinations:

- source of life energy: the interior world
- mode of assimilating information: via the senses

- decision-making mode: the mind
- lifestyle: organised

Similar personality types:

- the Practitioner
- the Administrator
- the Animator

Statistical data:

- *inspectors* constitute between six and ten per cent of the global community
- men predominate among *inspectors* (60 per cent)
- Switzerland is an example of a nation corresponding to the *inspector's* profile

Find out more!

The Inspector. Your Guide to the ISTJ Personality Type by Jaroslaw Jankowski

The Logician (INTP)

Life motto: Above all else, seek to discover the truths about the world.

Logicians are original, resourceful and creative. With a love for solving problems of a theoretical nature, they are analytical, quick-witted, enthusiastically disposed towards new concepts and have the ability to connect individual phenomena, educing general rules and theories from them. Logical, exact and inquiring, they are quick to spot incoherence and inconsistency.

Logicians are independent, sceptical of existing solutions and authorities, tolerant and open to new challenges. When immersed in thought, they will sometimes lose touch with the outside world.

The *logician's* four natural inclinations:

- source of life energy: the interior world
- mode of assimilating information: intuition
- decision-making mode: the mind
- lifestyle: spontaneous

Similar personality types:

- the Strategist
- the Innovator
- the Director

Statistical data:

- *logicians* constitute between two and three per cent of the global community;
- men predominate among *logicians* (80 per cent)
- India is an example of a nation corresponding to the *logician's* profile

Find out more!

The Logician. Your Guide to the INTP Personality Type by Jaroslaw Jankowski

The Mentor (INFJ)

Life motto: The world CAN be a better place!

Mentors are creative and sensitive. With their gaze fixed firmly on the future, they spot opportunities and potential imperceptible to others. Idealists and visionaries, they are geared towards helping people and are conscientious, responsible and, at one and the same time, courteous, caring and friendly. They strive to understand the mechanisms governing the world and view problems from a wide perspective.

Superb listeners and observers, *mentors* are characterised by their extraordinary empathy, intuition and trust of people and are capable of reading the feelings and emotions of others. They find criticism and conflict difficult to bear and can come across as enigmatic.

The *mentor's* four natural inclinations:

- source of life energy: the interior world
- mode of assimilating information: intuition
- decision-making mode: the heart
- lifestyle: organised

Similar personality types:

- the Idealist
- the Counsellor
- the Enthusiast

Statistical data:

- *mentors* constitute one per cent of the global community and are the most rarely occurring of the sixteen personality types

- women predominate among *mentors* (80 per cent)
- Norway is an example of a nation corresponding to the *mentor's* profile

Find out more!

The Mentor. Your Guide to the INFJ Personality Type by Jaroslaw Jankowski

The Practitioner (ISTP)

Life motto: Actions speak louder than words.

Practitioners are optimistic and spontaneous, with a positive approach to life. Reserved and independent, they hold true to their personal convictions and view external principles and norms with scepticism. They find abstract concepts and solutions for the future tiresome and would far rather roll up their sleeves and get to work on solving tangible and concrete problems.

Adapting well to new places and situations, they enjoy fresh challenges and risks and are capable of keeping a cool head in the face of threats and danger. Their general reticence and extreme reserve when it comes to expressing their opinions mean that other people may often find them impenetrable.

The *practitioner's* four natural inclinations:

- source of life energy: the interior world
- mode of assimilating information: via the senses

- decision-making mode: the mind
- lifestyle: spontaneous

Similar personality types:

- the Inspector
- the Animator
- the Administrator

Statistical data:

- *practitioners* constitute between six and nine per cent of the global community
- men predominate among *practitioners* (60 per cent)
- Singapore is an example of a nation corresponding to the *practitioner's* profile

Find out more!

The Practitioner. Your Guide to the ISTP Personality Type by Jaroslaw Jankowski

The Presenter (ESFP)

Life motto: Now is the perfect moment!

Presenters are optimistic, energetic and outgoing, with the ability to enjoy life and have fun to the full. Practical, flexible and spontaneous at one and the same time, they enjoy change and new experiences, coping badly with solitude, stagnation and routine.

With their liking for being at the centre of attention, they are natural-born actors and their speaking abilities arouse the interest and enthusiasm of their listeners. Focused as they are on the present moment, they will sometimes lose sight of their long-term aims and can also have problems with foreseeing the consequences of their actions.

The *presenter's* four natural inclinations:

- source of life energy: the exterior world
- mode of assimilating information: via the senses
- decision-making mode: the heart
- lifestyle: spontaneous

Similar personality types:

- the Advocate
- the Artist
- the Protector

Statistical data:

- *presenters* constitute between eight and thirteen per cent of the global community
- women predominate among *presenters* (60 per cent)
- Brazil is an example of a nation corresponding to the *presenter's* profile

Find out more!

The Presenter. Your Guide to the ESFP Personality Type by Jaroslaw Jankowski

The Protector (ISFJ)

Life motto: Your happiness matters to me.

Protectors are sincere, warm-hearted, unassuming, trustworthy and extraordinarily loyal. With their ability to perceive people's needs and their desire to help them, they will always put others first. Practical, well-organised and gifted with both an eye and a memory for detail, they are responsible, hard-working, patient, persevering and capable of seeing things through to the end.

Protectors set great store by tranquillity, stability and friendly relations with others and are skilled at building bridges between people. By the same token, they find conflict and criticism difficult to bear. Given their powerful sense of duty and their constant readiness to come to the aid of others, they can end up being used by people.

The *protector's* four natural inclinations:

- source of life energy: the interior world
- mode of assimilating information: via the senses
- decision-making mode: the heart
- lifestyle: organised

Similar personality types:

- the Artist
- the Advocate
- the Presenter

Statistical data:

- *protectors* constitute between eight and twelve per cent of the global population
- women predominate among *protectors* (70 per cent)
- Sweden is an example of a nation corresponding to the *protector's* profile

Find out more!

The Protector. Your Guide to the ISFJ Personality Type by Jaroslaw Jankowski

The Strategist (INTJ)

Life motto: I can certainly improve this.

Strategists are independent and outstandingly individualistic, with an immense seam of inner energy. Creative, inventive and resourceful, others perceive them as competent, self-assured and, at one and the same time, distant and enigmatic. No matter what they turn their attention to, they will always look at the bigger picture and they have a driving urge to improve the world around them and set it in order.

Well-organised, responsible, critical and demanding, they are difficult to knock off balance – and just as hard to please to the full. Reading the emotions and feelings of others is something they find very problematic.

The *strategist's* four natural inclinations:

- source of life energy: the interior world

- mode of assimilating information: intuition
- decision-making mode: the mind
- lifestyle: organised

Similar personality types:

- the Logician
- the Director
- the Innovator

Statistical data:

- *strategists* constitute between one and two per cent of the global community
- men predominate among *strategists* (80 per cent)
- Finland is an example of a nation corresponding to the *strategist's* profile

Find out more!

The Strategist. Your Guide to the INTJ Personality Type by Jaroslaw Jankowski

Additional information

The four natural inclinations

1. THE DOMINANT SOURCE OF LIFE
   ENERGY

   a. THE EXTERIOR WORLD
      People who draw their energy from
      outside. They need activity and contact
      with others and find being alone for
      any length of time hard to bear.

   b. THE INTERIOR WORLD
      People who draw their energy from
      their inner world. They need quiet and
      solitude and feel drained when they
      spend any length of time in a group.

2. THE DOMINANT MODE OF ASSIMILATING INFORMATION

    a. VIA THE SENSES
People who rely on the five senses and are persuaded by facts and evidence. They have a liking for methods and practices which are tried and tested and prefer concrete tasks and are realists who trust in experience.

    b. VIA INTUITION
People who rely on the sixth sense and are driven by what they 'feel in their bones'. They have a liking for innovative solutions and problems of a theoretical nature and are characterised by a creative approach to their tasks and the ability to predict.

3. THE DOMINANT DECISION-MAKING MODE

    a. THE MIND
People who are guided by logic and objective principles. They are critical and direct in expressing their opinions.

    b. THE HEART
People who are guided by their feelings and values. They long for harmony and mutual understanding with others.

4.   THE DOMINANT LIFESTYLE

   a.   ORGANISED
       People who are conscientious and
       organised. They value order and like to
       operate according to plan.

   b.   SPONTANEOUS
       People who are spontaneous and value
       freedom of action. They live for the
       moment and have no trouble finding
       their feet in new situations.

The approximate percentage of each personality type in the world population

Personality Type:	Proportion:
• The Administrator (ESTJ):	10-13%
• The Advocate (ESFJ):	10-13%
• The Animator (ESTP):	6-10%
• The Artist (ISFP):	6-9%
• The Counsellor (ENFJ):	3-5 %
• The Director (ENTJ):	2-5%
• The Enthusiast (ENFP):	5-8%
• The Idealist (INFP):	1-4%
• The Innovator (ENTP):	3-5%
• The Inspector (ISTJ):	6-10%
• The Logician (INTP):	2-3%
• The Mentor (INFJ):	ca. 1%
• The Practitioner (ISTP):	6-9%
• The Presenter (ESFP):	8-13%

- The Protector (ISFJ):   8-12%
- The Strategist (INTJ):   1-2%

The approximate percentage of women and men of each personality type in the world population

Personality Type: **Women / Men:**

- The Administrator (ESTJ):   40% / 60%
- The Advocate (ESFJ):   70% / 30%
- The Animator (ESTP):   40% / 60%
- The Artist (ISFP):   60% / 40%
- The Counsellor (ENFJ):   80% / 20%
- The Director (ENTJ):   30% / 70%
- The Enthusiast (ENFP):   60% / 40%
- The Idealist (INFP):   60% / 40%
- The Innovator (ENTP):   30% / 70%
- The Inspector (ISTJ):   40% / 60%
- The Logician (INTP):   20% / 80%
- The Mentor (INFJ):   80% / 20%
- The Practitioner (ISTP):   40% / 60%
- The Presenter (ESFP):   60% / 40%
- The Protector (ISFJ):   70% / 30%
- The Strategist (INTJ):   20% / 80%

Bibliography

- Arraj, Tyra & Arraj, James: *Tracking the Elusive Human, Volume 1: A Practical Guide to C.G. Jung's Psychological Types, W.H. Sheldon's Body and Temperament Types and Their Integration*, Inner Growth Books, 1988
- Arraj, James: *Tracking the Elusive Human, Volume 2: An Advanced Guide to the Typological Worlds of C. G. Jung, W.H. Sheldon, Their Integration, and the Biochemical Typology of the Future*, Inner Growth Books, 1990
- Berens, Linda V.; Cooper, Sue A.; Ernst, Linda K.; Martin, Charles R.; Myers, Steve; Nardi, Dario; Pearman, Roger R.; Segal, Marci; Smith, Melissa: *A Quick Guide to the 16 Personality Types in Organizations: Understanding Personality Differences in the Workplace*, Telos Publications, 2002
- Geier, John G. & Dorothy E. Downey: *Energetics of Personality*, Aristos Publishing House, 1989

- Geier, John G. & Downey, E. Dorothy: *Energetics of Personality*, Aristos Publishing House, 1989
- Hunsaker, Phillip L. & Alessandra, Anthony J.: *The Art of Managing People*, Simon and Schuster, 1986
- Kise, Jane A. G.; Stark, David & Krebs Hirsch, Sandra: *LifeKeys: Discover Who You Are*, Bethany House, 2005
- Kroeger, Otto & Thuesen, Janet: *Type Talk or How to Determine Your Personality Type and Change Your Life*, Delacorte Press, 1988
- Lawrence, Gordon: *People Types and Tiger Stripes*, Center for Applications of Psychological Type, 1993
- Lawrence, Gordon: *Looking at Type and Learning Styles*, Center for Applications of Psychological Type, 1997
- Maddi, Salvatore R.: *Personality Theories: A Comparative Analysis*, Waveland, 2001
- Martin, Charles R.: *Looking at Type: The Fundamentals Using Psychological Type To Understand and Appreciate Ourselves and Others*, Center for Applications of Psychological Type, 2001
- Meier C.A.: Personality: *The Individuation Process in the Light of C. G. Jung's Typology*, Daimon Verlag, 2007
- Pearman, Roger R. & Albritton, Sarah: *I'm Not Crazy, I'm Just Not You: The Real Meaning of the Sixteen Personality Types*, Davies-Black Publishing, 1997
- Segal, Marci: Creativity and Personality Type: *Tools for Understanding and Inspiring the Many Voices of Creativity*, Telos Publications, 2001

- Sharp, Daryl: Personality Type: *Jung's Model of Typology*, Inner City Books, 1987
- Spoto, Angelo: *Jung's Typology in Perspective*, Chiron Publications, 1995
- Tannen, Deborah: *You Just Don't Understand*, William Morrow and Company, 1990
- Thomas, Jay C. & Segal, Daniel L.: *Comprehensive Handbook of Personality and Psychopathology, Personality and Everyday Functioning*, Wiley, 2005
- Thomson, Lenore: *Personality Type: An Owner's Manual*, Shambhala, 1998
- Tieger, Paul D. & Barron-Tieger Barbara: *Just Your Type: Create the Relationship You've Always Wanted Using the Secrets of Personality Type*, Little, Brown and Company, 2000
- Von Franz, Marie-Louise & Hillman, James: *Lectures on Jung's Typology*, Continuum International Publishing Group, 1971

Putting the Reader first.

An Author Campaign Facilitated by ALLi.

www.ingramcontent.com/pod-product-compliance
Lightning Source LLC
Chambersburg PA
CBHW031208020426
42333CB00013B/849